The SOLWAY COAST – Powfoot to Caulkerbush

by
David Ca

Powfoot hasn't always been just a quiet coastal village. For many years its name was associated with Britain's chemical giant, ICI. ICI Powfoot was a very important employer in the area for over 50 years, and 3,000 or so people worked there after the old Ministry of Supply requisitioned Broom Farm following the outbreak of the Second World War. Initially managed by ICI's Nobel Division for the government, the plant formed part of a chain of munitions factories and depots in south-west Scotland. By the time operations ceased in March 1993, the workforce had dwindled to fewer than 100.

First published in the United Kingdom, 2002,
by Stenlake Publishing
Telephone / Fax: 01290 551122

ISBN 1 84033 215 8

FURTHER READING

The books listed below were used by the author during his research. None of them are available from Stenlake Publishing. Those interested in finding out more are advised to contact their local bookshop or reference library.

Blake, Brian, *The Solway Firth*, Robert Hale Ltd., 1955

Gifford, John, *The Buildings of Scotland: Dumfries and Galloway*, Penguin Books, 1996

Mackay, James A., *Burns–Lore of Dumfries and Galloway*, Alloway Publishing, 1988

Rowan, Alistair, *The Creation of Shambellie*, HMSO, 1982

AA Book of British Villages, Drive Publications, 1980

Through the Lens series (Nos. 17 & 21), Dumfries and Galloway Council

ACKNOWLEDGEMENT

I am particularly grateful to Bernadette Walsh, without whose help I would have been at a loss. This book is as much hers as mine.

The origins of the seventh or eighth century Ruthwell Cross are shrouded in mystery, and little is known of it except that the runic column was hewn from local stone and probably first served as a preaching cross; a place where people would gather for worship in the days before a church was built on the site. Eventually a church was constructed around the eighteen foot-high cross, but the column was destroyed as an 'idolatrous object' during the religious upheaval of Charles I's reign, and lay discarded in fragments until the importance of the remains was realised by Ruthwell's early nineteenth century minister, the Revd Henry Duncan. With the help of skilled craftsmen he restored the cross and, in 1823, it was erected in the garden of the manse. Sixty years later the column was painstakingly dismantled and re-erected inside the church, where it stands in all its restored glory. The panels are decorated and carved with scenes from the life of Christ and with lines from the Old English poem *The Dream of the Rood*.

INTRODUCTION

The officially designated Solway Coast Heritage Trail, along which tourists are guided by following the Celtic Cross symbol, extends for 190 miles from Annan to the Mull of Galloway. However, the part of the coastline which forms the geographical boundary of this book is slightly less ambitious, and stretches from Powfoot in the east to Caulkerbush in the west. With the exception of Dumfries, which punctuates the route midway, this is a thinly-populated region with almost uninterrupted views (weather permitting!) of the Lakeland fells on the opposite side of the Solway Firth.

Visitors who come to explore the part of the Solway Coast which is reflected in this volume, and who are attracted by the sequestered nature of the place, may be surprised to learn of its more hectic past: the huge ICI plant at Powfoot, for example, which was in existence until as recently as 1993, and – further along the coast – the once thriving Dumfries outposts of Glencaple and Carsethorn.

The Solway Coast is a magnet for fishermen and bird-watchers. The traditional art of haaf-netting is still practised in local waters while the flats and marshes of the Inner Solway abound with species of overwintering waterfowl. With the Royal Society for the Protection of Birds' reserve at Mersehead, and the National Nature Reserve at Caerlaverock, the seventh or eighth century Ruthwell Cross and the discovery of 'Mainsriddle Man', the coast offers much to interest not only the amateur naturalist, but the local historian and armchair archaeologist too.

The images that comprise this book (drawn largely from old postcards) reflect diverse aspects of the Solway Coast's interesting past: the time, for example, when plans were afoot to develop Powfoot and Cummertrees as a major holiday resort; the days when the cottage roofs of Mouswald and Bankend (and indeed other villages in the area) bore thatch rather than slate; and the time when Southerness was a simple coastal hamlet rather than the busy leisure village that it has become today. There are also reminders of the area's links with two of Scotland's greatest literary figures: Robert Burns and Sir Walter Scott. Burns spent a portion of his last days at Brow Well near Ruthwell, in what proved to be a hopeless quest for better health, while the model for Scott's 'Old Mortality' is buried in Caerlaverock churchyard.

A number of the photographs – the brooding hump of Criffel and the remains of Sweetheart Abbey; Caerlaverock Castle and the fast-flowing Nith – serve as reminders of just how little some things change over the years. We tend to think of the past and the present as two separate entities when, quite often, they are merely two different threads in one seamless tapestry – an apt thought, perhaps, with which to approach a volume of old photographs.

The Nith Hotel at Glencaple, with its excellent views of the Solway estuary, is a particularly suitable haunt for visitors with an interest in fishing and wildfowling. It is also a popular waterside retreat for the townspeople of nearby Dumfries seeking a meal and a drink. The hotel has always had something of a sporting flavour, and especially so since it was taken over more than 40 years ago by former Queen of the South and Scotland footballer, the late Billy Houliston. The hotel remains in the hands of the Houliston family and continues to have close links with the Queen of the South. In former times a Haaf Netters' Ball was held annually at the Nith Hotel to mark the end of the haaf-netting season.

Powfoot Golf Hotel looks across the Solway Firth to the Lakeland fells beyond. The hotel's Bunker and Smuggler's Bars are reminders of present and past pursuits in the area. With regard to the former, Powfoot Golf Club boasts a popular course in a most attractive location. The club was founded in 1903 when local laird, Edward Brook of Kinmount, laid out a course of nine holes which was extended to eighteen holes ten years later.

ELLERSLIE TERRACE, POWFOOT.

The spacious and well-designed Ellerslie Terrace, dating from the 1890s, was one of several similar housing developments that were built around the same time in Powfoot, and erected with the growth of the village as a holiday resort in mind. These substantial sandstone properties provide a considerable contrast both in size and style to Powfoot's older fishermen's cottages.

Lake View, Powfoot, was also built at the end of the nineteenth century.

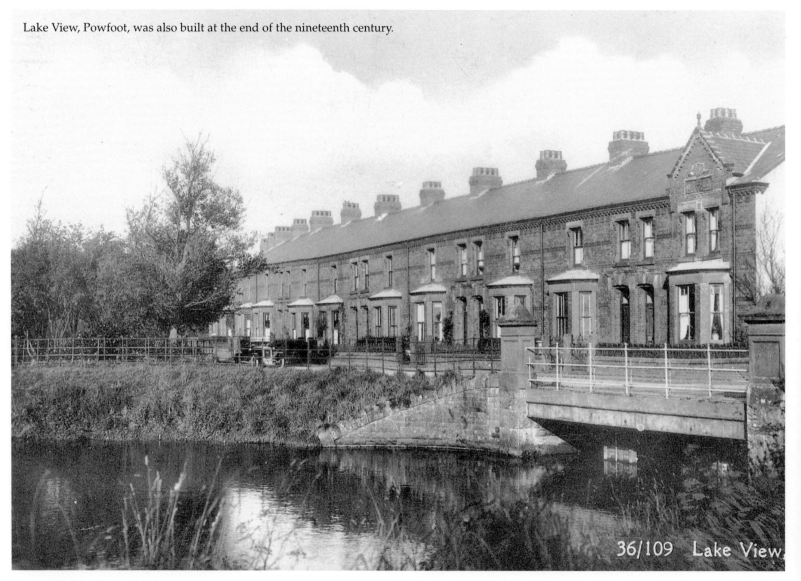

36/109 Lake View.

The fifteen eye-catching houses of Queensberry Terrace were built *c.*1900 by Edward Brook of Kinmount, again as part of the effort made around the beginning of the twentieth century to develop Cummertrees and Powfoot as a holiday resort. Recent architectural writers have described the terrace, with its subsequent additions and alterations, variously as 'a piece of seaside fun' and 'a cross between Blackpool and Chelsea'. The terrace stands out in sharp contrast to the traditional architectural style of the local area, and is a distinctive landmark lying on the outskirts of Cummertrees.

Cummertrees Church was built in 1777 and refurbished in the 1870s, with more interior renovation work carried out during the 1920s. The lych-gate is perhaps one of its most interesting features. Not only is its design unusual for the area, but it was built as a form of war memorial, in tribute to the men of the parish who died in action during the First and Second World Wars.

Cummertrees station dates from c.1848 and the opening of the Glasgow, Dumfries and Carlisle railway line. This was just one of several routes to be constructed in the area around that time of nationwide railway development, another of which was the fondly-remembered (and still sadly missed) 'Paddy Line', which conveyed passengers to and from the Irish ferry at Stranraer, and which also connected with the Caledonian Railway route to Glasgow and the south at Gretna junction. Cummertrees station was closed in September 1955, and nowadays trains speed through the village without even slowing down en route between Dumfries and Annan. The former station house, built of red sandstone, is now a private dwelling.

Ruthwell village and its surroundings were described over 70 years ago by former local minister John L. Dinwiddie as 'a typical example of a Dumfriesshire seaside parish'. Thirty years ago the *Dumfries and Galloway Standard*, in reflective mood, waxed lyrical over the same area. 'If one travels by car or cycles along its quiet lanes, passing through Ruthwell village . . . one cannot fail to feel the positive presence of Peace. This is not just the absence of noise and traffic; it is an influence breathed by the whole surrounding scene – the lush green meadows, the browsing cattle, the roadside blossom, and the wide sky and sea.' Most people who visit the area would agree that this description is as apt today as it was when it was written. On a sombre note, seventeen people from Ruthwell died in 1627 while gathering the salt harvest in local Solway waters; they were caught in a sudden high tide and drowned.

Ruthwell Church is the home of the Ruthwell Cross (page 2). The church's most illustrious minister was the Revd Henry Duncan, a Lochrutton man of many parts. He served this windswept Solway parish energetically and well from 1799 until 1843 and – in addition to restoring the runic preaching cross and founding the savings banks movement – he was also a distinguished geologist. He made the earliest British study of fossil footprints, working from a slab of red sandstone which had been recovered from the Corncockle Muir quarry near Templand (north-west of Lockerbie). When Duncan presented his findings to the Royal Society in Edinburgh in 1829 it proved to be the first scientific account of its kind.

The Revd Henry Duncan (inset) is probably best remembered as the founding father of the savings banks movement, which began when he opened his first ledger on 10 May 1810 in the cottage seen here on the right, at one end of Ruthwell's main street. Members (mainly agricultural workers in this rural parish) paid in quarterly subscriptions to the society, in return for which they were entitled to such benefits as sick pay and funeral grants. The premises are now home to the tiny Savings Banks Museum, which was opened in 1974 to coincide with the bicentenary of Henry Duncan's birth, and which in recent years has attracted well over 3,000 visitors annually. The exhibits are arranged in the room where Duncan used to receive his parishioners' savings, and they also reflect his other interests as publisher, author and geologist. Ruthwell's savings bank closed in 1876, when all the accounts were transferred to the Annan branch.

Brow Well (foreground) is situated a mile or so west of Ruthwell. Burns spent two weeks here at the end of his life, taking the waters and bathing in the Solway on the advice of his doctor, in what ultimately proved to be a futile attempt to revive his rapidly failing health. He died less than a week after returning to his home in Dumfries. Inevitably, Brow Well has become an essential port-of-call for anyone with an interest in Burns's life and work. On 17 July 1996 (a few days before the 200th anniversary of the poet's death), a large crowd of people attended the bicentenary commemorative service that was held here, on the edge of the Solway.

A nineteenth century view of the fourteenth century keep of Comlongon Castle, Clarencefield. Comlongon was built on the shores of the Solway in a bid to foil the frequent raids taking place at that time from the English side of the border. Nowadays, the 70-foot high keep – which, with its dungeons and restored Great Hall is considered one of the most impressive examples of its kind remaining in southern Scotland – adjoins a Scottish Baronial-style mansion which serves as a hotel, set at the end of a mile-long drive in 120 acres of grounds.

Looking west along Clarencefield's main street. The village, which stands midway along the old road between Dumfries and Annan, has swollen in size since the Second World War and now consists of a mixture of modern (mainly bungalow) and traditional housing styles. The stone cottages seen here on the right remain, leading to the Farmer's Inn further along the street. Brow Well is nearby (a footpath leads to it from the main street), reminding any Burnsian that when the poet came to take the waters of the well during the last few weeks of his life, Clarencefield was the place where he reputedly proffered his seal in lieu of cash to the local innkeeper as payment for a bottle of port (which he had been recommended to drink for medicinal purposes).

Looking west along Carrutherstown's main street in the years before the Second World War. Until recent years the village was situated on the main road between Dumfries and Annan, but it has now been bypassed. Cycling became an immensely popular pursuit during the early years of the twentieth century and roadside stops for refreshments were an integral part of the day's outing. Carrutherstown had its popular Cyclists' Rest in the cottage in the right foreground, now a private dwelling. Food and accommodation can still be obtained in the village at the recently refurbished Carrutherstown Hotel.

Hetland Hall, situated a mile or so west of Carrutherstown with views across the Solway, was built in 1868 and served for many years as a private country mansion. As recently as the 1960s it was used as a seminary, before being turned into the Hetland Hall Hotel which is familiar to visitors today. To the casual observer the exterior of the building does not seem to have altered dramatically over the years, but the original owners of this elegant property – were they able to return – would be astonished to find that it now boasts its own helicopter landing pad for the convenience of guests!

Were the football commentator John Motson reporting on Mouswald, lying between the A75 trunk road and the old road from Annan to Dumfries, he might perhaps be tempted to describe it as a village of two halves, although 'scattered' would be the better adjective. The nucleus of the community is presided over by the parish church, with its outlying satellites embracing the nineteenth century village school, the late-eighteenth century Mouswald Grange with its earlier (c.1700) windmill tower, and what is now the Mouswald Park caravan site. The thatched roofs seen in this early twentieth century photograph have all gone – thatch was in the process of being replaced by slate at the time – although a few of the village's older cottages have been improved and remain. Much of the current housing stock, however, dates from the twentieth century.

Mouswald Church stands at the junction of the village's main street and the old Annan to Dumfries road. It was built in 1816 and refurbished in 1929. Visitors exploring the church today will find that, among the work carried out at that time, was the rebuilding of the belfry which is now capped in a different style with the bell enclosed. Also, the side walls of the church now contain three windows of Gothic design instead of two.

Gillespie Memorial Hall, Mouswald.

The Gillespie Memorial Hall, Mouswald. This grey and somewhat plain building is named after the Revd John Gillespie, Mouswald's minister from 1865 to 1912. Now in the hands of Dumfries and Galloway Council's Department of Community Resources, it stands at the heart of local community life, and is used for a wide range of activities from mother and toddler groups to annual Burns suppers.

Cleughbrae, situated beside the busy A75 at Mouswald, has been so completely refashioned since this nineteenth-century photograph was taken as to be all but unrecognisable, with the bungalow-style building pictured here having been transformed into a two-storey dwelling. Cleughbrae was formerly the home of Robert Corsane Reid, a long-serving local politician and dedicated local historian, who died in the early 1960s.

A nineteenth-century view of Bankend village, north of Caerlaverock Castle, showing many of the stone cottages with their original thatched roofs. In a fascinating history of the district, prepared by members of Glencaple Women's Rural Institute during the 1960s, it is recorded that a detachment of the Jacobite army, led by Prince Charlie himself, passed through Bankend in late 1745 on its way north after fleeing from Derby. 'According to popular tradition he stayed at Townhead, Bankend', the WRI account explains, 'while some of his men stayed at a house in the village occupied by the Mathieson family, where bannocks were specially baked for them'.

Kirkconnel Lea, Caerlaverock, was formerly the home of Major General James Scott-Elliot, a man of diverse accomplishments who died in 1996 at the age of 93. A Commander of the 8th Battalion Argyll and Sutherland Highlanders during the Second World War, he became a celebrated dowser after retiring from the army. His book, *Dowsing: One Man's Way*, which was privately printed in 1977, attracted so much attention that it was reissued commercially two years later. Major General Scott-Elliot was Lord Lieutenant of Dumfriesshire from 1962 until 1967.

Caerlaverock Castle is situated south-east of Dumfries. Standing close to the Solway shore and at the mouth of the River Nith, this ancient stronghold of the Maxwells (who first built a castle at Caerlaverock in the early thirteenth century) was the 'Ellangowan' of Sir Walter Scott's novel *Guy Mannering*. The castle presides over the Caerlaverock National Nature Reserve, the largest wetland reserve in Britain, established in 1957. Here, also, is the Wildfowl and Wetlands Trust's centre at Eastpark (one of nine such centres in Britain) where the local wildlife can be viewed from hides, towers and a heated observatory. As the WWT's Caerlaverock publicity leaflet boasts, every month brings fresh fascination.

31 GLENCAPLE VILLAGE, NEAR DUMFRIES.

The riverside village of Glencaple, about four miles south of Dumfries, is now home to the Nith Inshore Rescue Boat. In the days when Dumfries was a bustling port, however, Glencaple served as an outport, situated at the spot where the Nith begins to widen and flow into the Solway Firth. Glencaple Quay was built in 1746, with Kingholm Quay, a few miles upstream (another port of call en route to Dumfries), being constructed the following year.

Glencaple has been more fortunate than many small rural communities in retaining its village post office up to the present time, although it (and the village stores) have shifted one cottage to the left since this photograph was taken.

The 3rd King's Own Scottish Borderers passing close by the River Nith as they enter Glencaple from the north in the early 1900s. In the days before army recruitment centres were a familiar feature on Britain's high streets, local regimental recruitment marches were often held around the country, visiting towns and surrounding villages in a bid to attract new recruits. The soldiers, kitted out for the occasion in their finest regimental uniforms, together with the stirring military music that accompanied them, would have made a great impression on the small communities they visited en route (as here, at Glencaple), and no doubt more than one impressionable young man was tempted to take the King's Shilling before the day was out (and perhaps bitterly regretted it the next morning!).

Haaf netting at Glencaple. In this age-old method of fishing the waters of the Solway the participants form a human chain or line, with their nets attached to poles in front of them, and by these means intercept and catch their fish. Brian Blake, writing in *The Solway Firth* (1955), explains that 'to do the job properly requires a good constitution and strong wrists, a quick mind, an X-ray eye and an intimate knowledge of the Solway shores'.

This picture is reproduced from a postcard entitled 'The Solway's fast flowing tide passing Glencaple'. 'Love swells like the Solway / But ebbs like its tide', wrote Sir Walter Scott, mindful perhaps of the age-old local saying that, 'The tide sweeps into the Solway as fast as a galloping horse' (as many unfortunate souls have discovered to their cost over the years). Not only the Solway's tides, but its shifting sands too, are perilous as Scott darkly hinted in *Redgauntlet*. 'Those that dream on the Solway may wake up in another world', he warned.

The village of Kelton, situated on the edge of the River Nith between Glencaple and Dumfries, photographed *c*.1910. In 1792 the smuggling vessel *Rosamond* was repaired at a boatyard here after it had been seized by Robert Burns and his fellow excisemen during an incident at Sarkfoot near Gretna. Kelton is still a peaceful riverside hamlet today, despite lying only a few miles south of Dumfries.

The estate of Kirkconnell has been held by the Maxwells and their descendants since the early fifteenth century, and lies between New Abbey and the west bank of the River Nith. The present Kirkconnell House was built in the mid-eighteenth century by James Maxwell, whose son William was not only one of Burns's closest friends, but as a general practitioner working in Dumfries was also the poet's medical adviser. Writing in his *Burns–Lore of Dumfries and Galloway* (1988), James A. Mackay notes that 'the Maxwells of Kirkconnell were deeply pious and generous benefactors of the Church. After the Reformation they remained steadfast to the old faith, their sons often being educated at the Scots College in Douai, Flanders.'

Shambellie House lies on the outskirts of New Abbey. The property – described in a guidebook to the house as 'a Scottish Baronial Mansion on a modest scale' – was designed by architect David Bryce and built for the Stewart Family in 1856 at a cost of something under £3,000. For more than a century Shambellie served as a private residence until, in 1977, the house and its owner's costume collection were given to the National Museums of Scotland. As Shambellie House Museum of Costume it is now open to the public from April to October, and a tour through its various rooms provides an opportunity to view different aspects of the clothes collection in a variety of fully furnished domestic settings over a period from c.1860 to 1930.

The Solway Fishery at New Abbey was founded by J. J. Armistead during the 1870s. Still thriving today, the fishery is thought to be one of the oldest, perhaps even *the* oldest, in Britain. Although fish had been farmed and cultivated for centuries using primitive methods, Armistead, an energetic Victorian entrepreneur, was one of the first people to recognise the commercial possibilities of the operation. 'When I commenced the work', he explained in *The Gallovidian* in 1899, 'but little was known of the rearing of fish after they were hatched . . . Many difficulties had to be bridged over, and it was only by the most persevering attention and constant study of the requirements of the delicate little creatures with which we had to deal that success was at last attained'. From New Abbey, Armistead exported fish ova wrapped in moss as far afield as New Zealand.

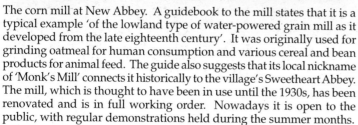

The corn mill at New Abbey. A guidebook to the mill states that it is a typical example 'of the lowland type of water-powered grain mill as it developed from the late eighteenth century'. It was originally used for grinding oatmeal for human consumption and various cereal and bean products for animal feed. The guide also suggests that its local nickname of 'Monk's Mill' connects it historically to the village's Sweetheart Abbey. The mill, which is thought to have been in use until the 1930s, has been renovated and is in full working order. Nowadays it is open to the public, with regular demonstrations held during the summer months.

There is a decidedly romantic air about the ruins of Sweetheart Abbey, particularly when they are bathed in early morning sunshine or cloaked in the shadows of a summer's evening. Perhaps it is the manner in which the rich red sandstone catches and responds to the light, or perhaps these remains have simply absorbed into their fabric something of their romantic origins. The thirteenth century Cistercian abbey was founded by Lady Devorgilla in memory of her husband John Balliol. Legend has it that she was so devoted to him she had his heart placed in a small box and kept it with her always. On her own death in 1289 she was buried along with her husband's heart in the abbey (thus 'Sweetheart Abbey').

There is an almost suburban air to the gabled Commercial Inn, pictured here on one side of The Square in New Abbey. Nowadays it is called the Criffel Arms, presumably in homage to the mountain under which the village shelters.

On the opposite side of The Square from the former Commercial Inn stands the Abbey Arms Hotel, its name a reminder of the Cistercian remains that loom up at the other end of New Abbey. Thus can be found in close proximity the sacred and the secular, linked by the narrow main street which can prove a formidable bottleneck for traffic in the crowded tourist season.

Looking along New Abbey's narrow main street, with the remains of Sweetheart Abbey forming a towering backdrop. Apart from the fact that the houses seen here have been much improved since this photograph was taken in the early 1900s, this tight aperture (on the now busy route between Dumfries and the Solway Coast) is instantly recognisable as the present-day village. One of the single-storey cottages on the left often causes visitors to pause and wonder. Set into its front wall is a simple stone carving of a boat with three occupants, all picked out in colour against the whitewashed background. It is said to commemorate the tireless efforts of three women who reputedly worked long and hard during the building of the abbey by transporting red sandstone across the Solway.

Pupils photographed outside New Abbey school on George V's Coronation Day, 22 June 1911. In the morning the children gathered in the village square and took part in a large procession, led by a pipe band, to the parish church, where a service was held to mark the occasion. Later, the children were given a lunch at Shambellie and presented with Coronation mugs. 'Despite the unfavourable weather conditions the inhabitants of New Abbey celebrated the Coronation with much enthusiasm', reported the local newspaper. 'The houses in the village were gaily bedecked with flags and streamers, and the day was given up to enjoyment.'

NEW ABBEY PARISH CHURCH.

The thriving parish church of New Abbey, set in peaceful and secluded surroundings on the edge of the village, is described by John Gifford in his *Buildings of Scotland: Dumfries and Galloway* (1996) as 'mechanical Gothic' in style. Designed by James Barbour, it was built of grey granite in the late 1870s.

The stone-built Waterloo Monument, erected in 1815 to commemorate the 'Iron Duke's' famous victory against the French, stands on a hilltop near New Abbey and in the shadow of Criffel. Anyone with a good head for heights and an energetic disposition can climb the monument's steep spiral staircase, and gain from the column's open-air top a stunning bird's-eye view (on a clear day, at least!) over the surrounding countryside and Solway Firth.

WATERLOO MONUMENT, NEW ABBEY,
ERECTED IN THE YEAR 1815 TO COMMEMORATE
WELLINGTON'S VICTORY.

The towering hump of Criffel, seen here from Loch Kindar on the outskirts of New Abbey. There is more than one way to reach Criffel's summit of *c.*1,869 feet. My favourite route follows the steep – and in wet weather very muddy – ascent of Knockendoch, from where there is the bonus of a comparatively easy ridge walk to be enjoyed, leading to the top of the higher peak. The panoramic views afforded by Criffel's summit easily repay the effort of reaching it. Despite the hill's proximity to Dumfries, its slopes – unlike those of the crowded Lakeland fells just across the Solway – are often surprisingly deserted, even on a fine day. A local rhyme declares that 'When Criffel wears his hat / Ye may be sure it will be wat / But if instead he wears his tie / Ye may expect it to be dry'.

Carsethorn, *c*.1925. Situated on the coast at the point where the River Nith flows into the Solway Firth, Carsethorn was a thriving outport serving Dumfries during the eighteenth century; a place from where countless numbers of people emigrated to the 'New World', and where vessels that were too large to navigate the Nith were able to unload their cargoes. (The former name of Carsethorn's present-day 'Steamboat' – the Ship Inn – recalls those times). The village, resting in the shadow of Criffel in an area dubbed 'the garden of Galloway', is now a popular spot for visitors.

Arbigland House, Kirkbean, in the early 1900s. Brian Blake, writing in *The Solway Firth* (1955) describes how in the eighteenth century the estate's owner, William Craik, became the first president of the Society for the Improvement of Agriculture in South-West Scotland. Craik was 'a good practical farmer', explains Blake, 'and a leader in the application of new ideas. He was probably one of the first to use the English plough in place of the cumbersome Scottish one.' On a literary note, it was here at Arbigland that Burns met Anna Benson, a lady who long after the poet's death described him in a letter to Thomas Carlyle's wife, Jane, as 'incapable of rudeness or vulgarity . . . well bred and gentlemanly in all the courtesies of life'.

John Paul Jones, the so-called father of the American Navy, was born in this simple stone cottage on the Arbigland Estate, Kirkbean, in July 1747. The cottage was built by Arbigland's mid-eighteenth century owner, William Craik, to house the family of the estate's head gardener, a post filled at that time by Jones's father. Jones earned his sobriquet after working tirelessly in the United States and persuading the authorities there to raise their standards of maritime training and efficiency; a crusade that was eventually to bear fruit with the founding of the Annapolis Naval College. The cottage, set in secluded country close to the water's edge, was opened in July 1993 as the John Paul Jones Birthplace Museum, and now attracts over 1,000 visitors each summer. The interior, with its low-beamed ceilings and stone-flagged floors, has been expertly recreated to impersonate the mid-eighteenth century style of Jones's childhood.

Kirkbean village (seen here with Criffel in the background) lies on the A710 between New Abbey and Caulkerbush. In addition to John Paul Jones, the parish nurtured another famous seafaring son: Admiral John Campbell who, between 1740 and 1744 circumnavigated the globe with the English naval commander George Anson. Cavens, on the outskirts of the village, is now a hotel but the estate and mansion were owned by the Oswald family in the eighteenth century. James A. Mackay records that Robert Burns visited the Oswalds here, and was much struck by the beauty of Richard Oswald's wife, Lucy.

The coastal hamlet of Southerness juts out into the Solway Firth, and when this photograph was taken in the 1930s it consisted of little more than these two rows of stone cottages, which face each other across the narrow road that leads down towards the shore and lighthouse. The large house in the centre has since been much altered and transformed into the John Paul Jones Hotel. The village was originally named Salterness (on account of the salt harvest that was once gathered in local waters) and the name corrupted to Southerness in the late-nineteenth century.

A view of Southerness taken from its lighthouse during the 1960s. The hamlet's old cottages remain, but already in this picture there is evidence of the caravans which have subsequently grown vastly in number and have transformed this hitherto quiet spot into a popular holiday resort on the Solway. Now, however, in addition to the fields stretching away into the distance there are golf courses, a leisure park and a holiday village with acres of holiday homes, together with all the usual attendant facilities, including an amusement arcade, heated indoor swimming pool, adventure playground for children and live entertainment.

Children enjoying the sea air at the appropriately named Hutland, at Gillfoot near Southerness. Simple wooden cottages and chalets of the type seen here were a familiar feature of coastal resorts around the country in the post-Second World War era. They served either as second homes for townspeople in search of a weekend retreat, or provided basic self-catering accommodation for those seeking an independent seaside holiday and a more convenient alternative to bed-and-breakfast or hotel accommodation (in the days before most of us spent our holidays abroad). The long-term future of the properties pictured here on Gillfoot Farm would always have been in the hands of the gods, given the vigorous south-westerlies that pile into the Solway Firth from the Irish Sea and, predictably, a number of these wooden buildings came to grief after taking a particularly heavy pounding from bad weather in the 1960s.

If you happen to blink while driving through Mainsriddle, a quiet hamlet straddling the road between Kirkbean and Caulkerbush, there is a sporting chance that you will miss it. Proving that size isn't everything, however, Mainsriddle boasts an attractive garden centre / nursery and also a pottery, making it an interesting port-of-call for anyone following the Solway Coast tourist route. The former inn (pictured here in its heyday) is now a private house.

Probably one of the more remarkable events to disturb the even tenor of the peaceful backwater of Mainsriddle (named, incidentally, after Sir James Riddell, a former local landowner), occurred during the years following the Second World War, when the remains of a Bronze Age man were unearthed nearby. Dubbed 'Mainsriddle Man', this important archaeological discovery may be viewed by visitors to Dumfries museum.

Cattle grazing in the grounds of Southwick House, north-east of Caulkerbush village, in the early 1900s. James A. Mackay records that in the late-eighteenth century the mansion was owned by Lieutenant-General Dunlop, MP for the Stewartry between 1813 and 1826 and the son of one of Burns's greatest friends, Mrs Frances Dunlop. When this photograph was taken Southwick House was the home of Sir Mark John MacTaggart Stewart Bart., who died in September 1923. There is a memorial to him in nearby Southwick Church.

Caulkerbush is situated on the A710 north-west of Southerness. The stone bridge over Boreland Burn, beyond the gabled houses on the left, was originally built in 1789 but was demolished, widened and rebuilt in 1999 with aid from the European Regional Development Fund in order to ease the traffic flow. The grey stone parish church, built in 1891, lies a short distance to the north of the village, while to the south can be found the Mersehead Nature Reserve. The RSPB acquired Mersehead in 1993 and many visitors are attracted to this part of the Solway, where large numbers of various bird species roost, including barnacle geese, oystercatchers and the quaintly-named bartailed godwit.